Ahmadu Bamba
Sage of Senegal

A Coloring Storybook

By Rukayat Yakub

The Blessed Prophet Muhammad, the Prophet of love and mercy, lived and taught the Oneness of God in Mecca, Arabia. In the early days of his mission, due to the harsh treatment by the people of Mecca, many of his followers fled to the Empire of Axum in East Africa.

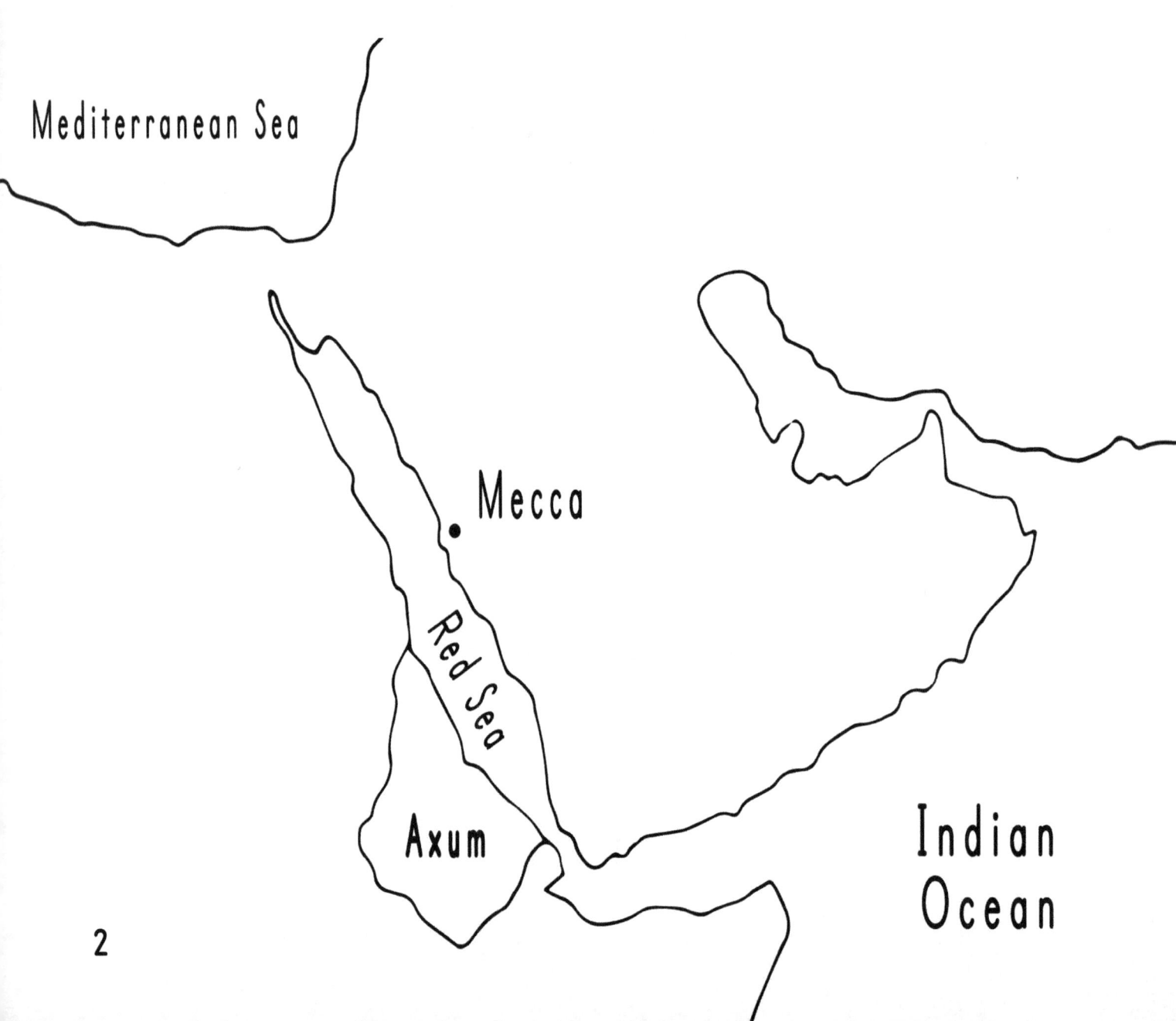

Over time, his teachings spread to the kingdoms of West Africa as well. He taught people to live in loving surrender to God, their creator and caretaker.

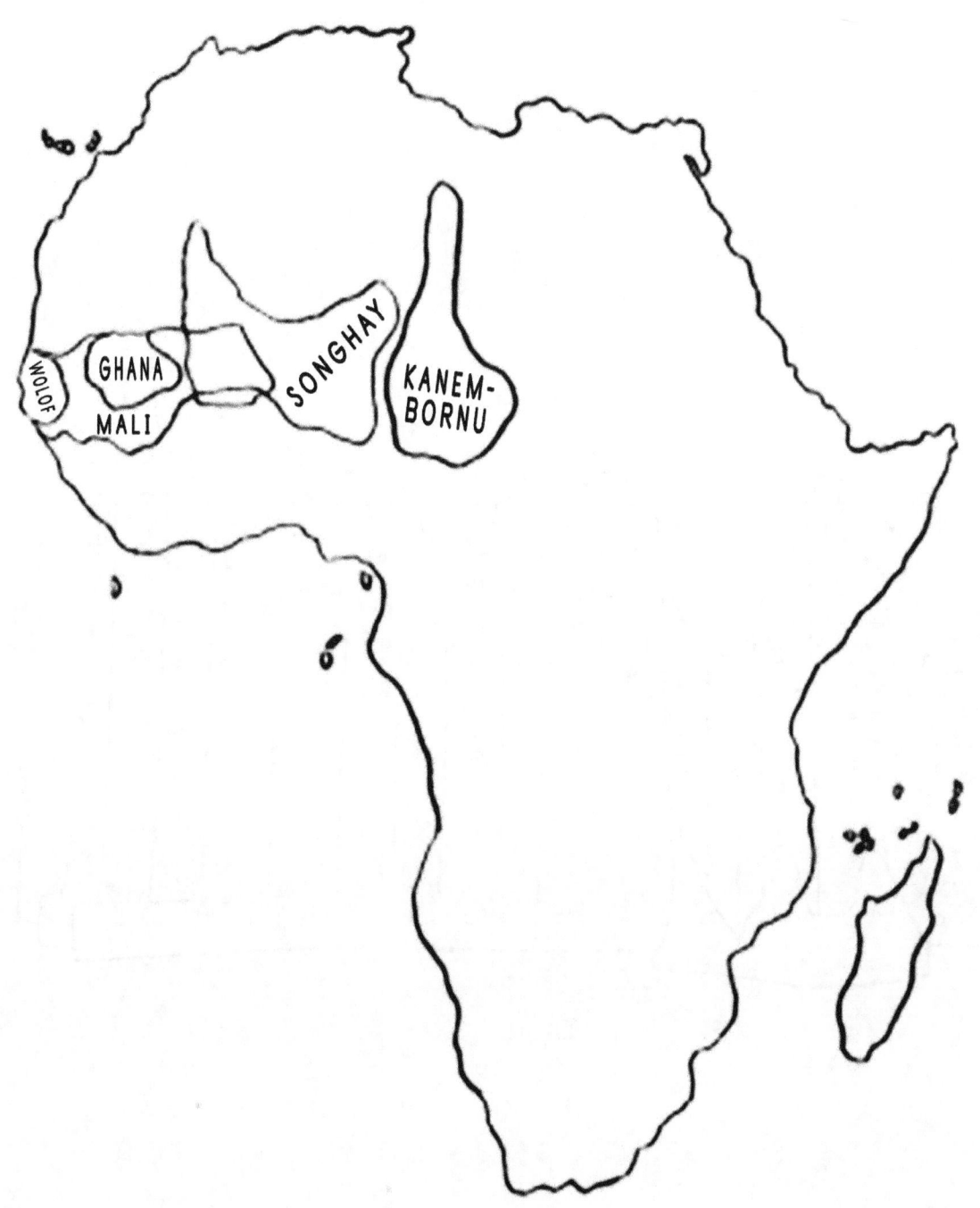

African Muslims built schools, mosques, and universities across the region, like the Grand Mosque of Djenné.

At the edge of West Africa lies Senegal. It is a land of books, generosity, warmth, and above all, a love of God.

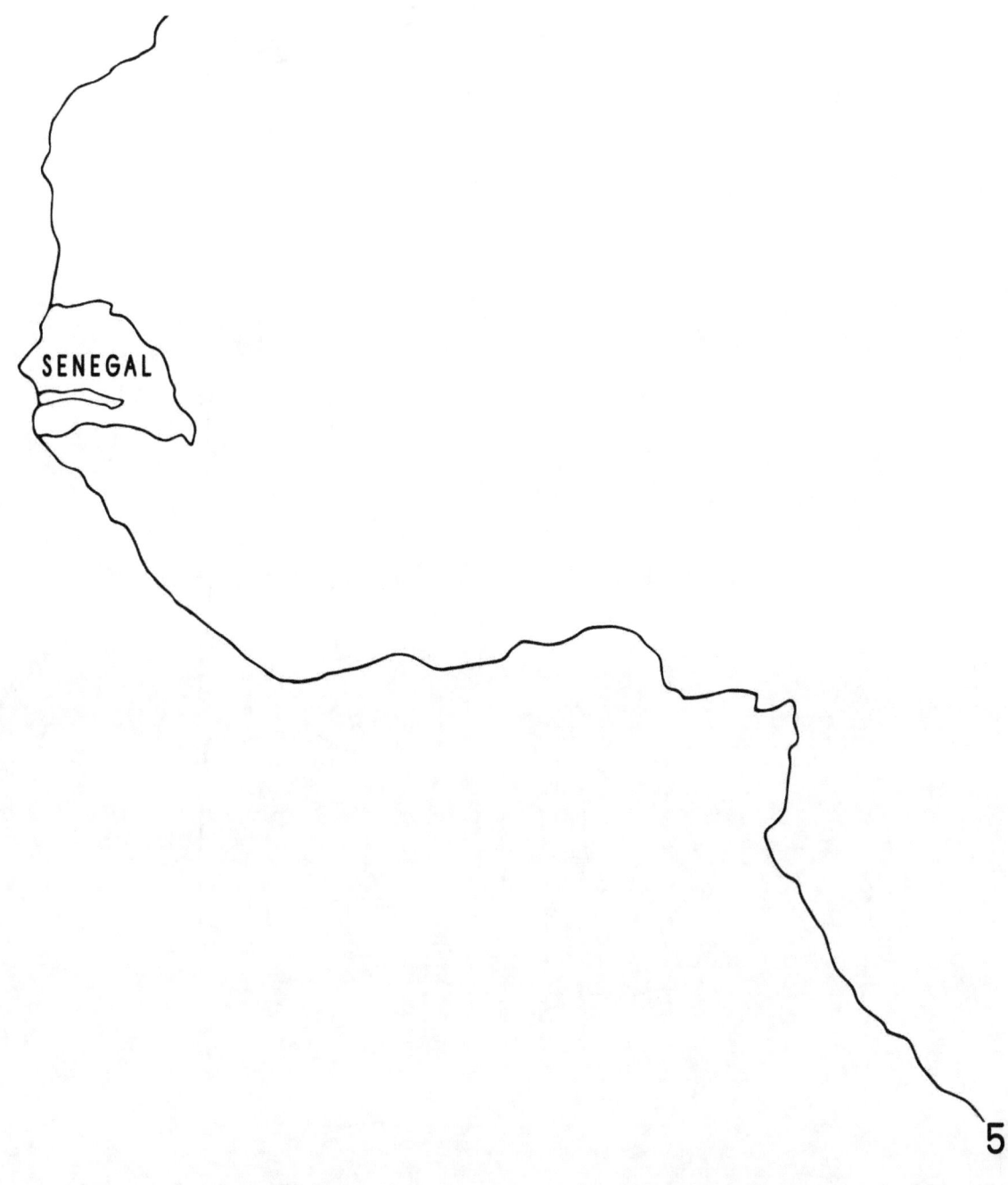

In 1853, a child was born in this very land – a child who would grow up to become the great Ahmadu Bamba. His mother, Lady Mariama Bousso, was a pious, kind, hardworking scholar.

In the middle of the night, young Ahmadu would stand on a soft lambskin prayer rug surrounded by the moonlit stones that marked out the prayer area of the family compound. At a young age he wished to be like the people of God who stand at night in prayer.

Ahmadu, like most of the children of his time, started to memorize the Qur'an when he was about 6 years old. He loved it! He studied Qur'an with his Granduncle Ndumbe, his father Momar, and his uncle Muhammad. He completed his memorization at the age of 12 using a wooden tablet and reed pen.

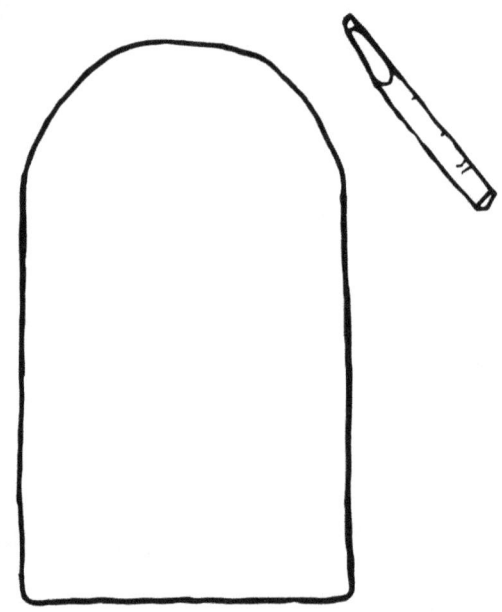

After he finished the first stage of his education, he studied the Arabic language, Islamic law, Sirah (Life of the Blessed Prophet), and his favorite, Poetry. Ahmadu would carry his precious books in a beautiful satchel.

By the age of 20, Ahmadu was called Shaykh Bamba, out of respect for his learning. Now he was teaching at his father's academy. Shaykh Bamba also wrote many books, some of which are shown below in the great Library of Touba, Senegal.

When Shaykh Bamba was 30, Elder Mandumbe invited him to be part of the king's court. He said to him, "Work for the king and you will receive gifts that will fulfill all your needs!" Shaykh Bamba replied, "No, I will not rely on kings. I am satisfied with God, so I put my trust in Him."

Shaykh Bamba helped his people become independent through farming, hard work, and faith. He and his students established cities like Dar-us-Salaam, then Touba, where he laid the foundations of the Grand Mosque.

He showed his people just how much power they truly had. This worried not only the local leaders but also the French colonizers. Eventually, he was called to court, before the Privy Council.

The Council quickly decided to exile Shaykh Bamba to Mayumba, Gabon. The Shaykh was to be placed on a ship and forced to leave Senegal. In a few days, Shaykh Bamba would have to leave his home, his family, and his students forever!

But instead of taking him to his cell to await exile to Gabon, the guards hatched a plan. Thinking there must be a quicker way to get rid of him, they threw the Shaykh into a cell with a starving lion.

However, when they returned, the once ferocious lion was as gentle as a lamb.

Soon after, the Shaykh was shackled and placed on a ship.

Find Dakar, Conakry, Grand Bassam, Cotonou, Douala, Libreville and Mayumba on the map. Next, connect these coastal cities to trace the Shaykh's exile route.

14

On the voyage to Libreville the Shaykh was stopped from praying on the ship, so he cast out a prayer rug and miraculously prayed on the ocean, through the power of God.

Draw in the prayer rug and decorate it any way you like.

The Shaykh was left on the island of Mayumba with his belongings. No one had ever returned, so his enemies thought this was the end of him at last!

However, the Shaykh lived. He spent most of his time in prayer and writing. He wrote lots of books while in exile.

After seven years, the French decided to return him to Senegal. The crowd could barely wait to catch a glimpse of the great Shaykh Bamba when the ship came to shore.

After his return, Shaykh Bamba said, "I love God so much that I can't be angry at the people who tried to hurt me. I forgive them all."

For the rest of his life, Shaykh Bamba continued to teach, write, and show people how to live a life of peace, love, and hard work.

Today, people from around the world are inspired by Shaykh Bamba's life and millions visit Touba and pray in the mosque that he lay the foundations for many years ago.

Try to draw Shaykh Bamba.

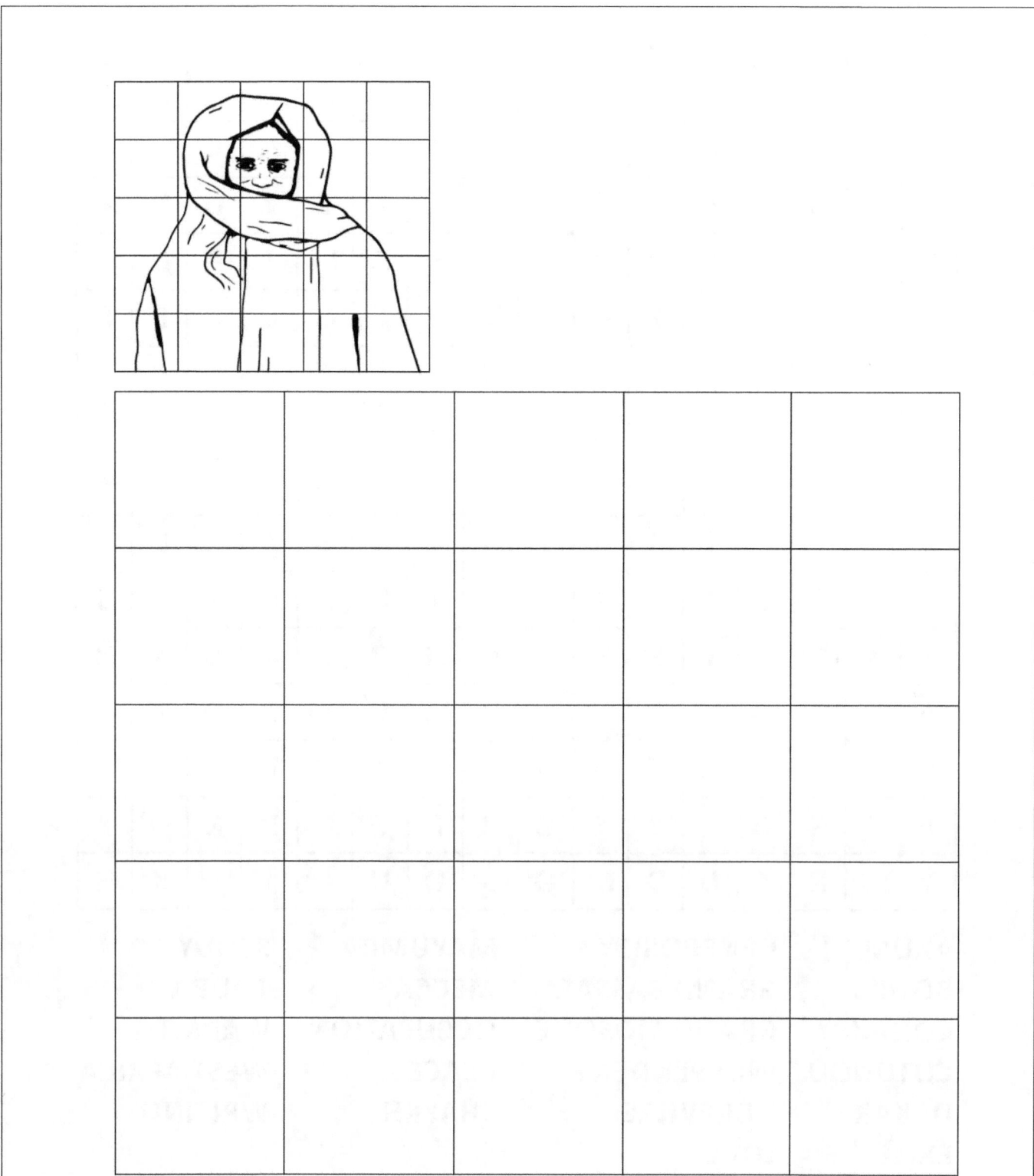

Find the words below in this word search.

L	I	B	R	E	V	I	L	L	E	R	P	T	N	B	W
A	I	C	W	I	A	I	C	W	I	A	E	C	O	I	E
M	A	Y	U	M	B	A	D	C	G	X	A	D	C	G	S
R	B	W	U	R	M	E	C	C	A	D	C	A	C	I	T
A	I	A	Z	L	C	V	A	E	A	Z	E	Z	U	N	A
X	G	R	A	N	D	B	A	S	S	A	M	I	P	D	F
U	T	M	E	G	G	U	N	T	P	E	G	G	A	E	R
M	R	T	E	P	E	C	P	U	Y	E	T	R	T	P	I
R	U	H	B	W	N	O	H	D	R	S	O	O	I	E	C
L	C	A	R	R	E	N	S	Y	N	T	U	S	O	N	A
O	K	I	O	I	R	A	I	S	I	O	B	A	N	D	I
V	E	R	O	T	O	K	C	C	I	D	A	N	T	E	S
E	X	N	R	I	S	R	O	E	H	R	F	P	B	N	H
A	I	O	W	N	I	Y	N	D	A	K	A	R	O	T	A
P	L	I	G	G	T	A	W	C	O	T	O	N	O	U	Y
P	E	N	G	L	Y	T	O	R	P	G	O	D	K	O	K
Y	G	R	A	N	D	M	O	S	Q	U	E	I	S	K	H

AXUM   **GENEROSITY**   **MAYUMBA**   **STUDY**
BOOKS   **GRAND BASSAM**   **MECCA**   **TOUBA**
CONAKRY   **GRAND MOSQUE**   **OCCUPATION**   **WARMTH**
COTONOU   **INDEPENDENT**   **PEACE**   **WEST AFRICA**
DAKAR   **LIBREVILLE**   **SHAYKH**   **WRITING**
EXILE   **LOVE**

Find the way to the Grand Mosque of Djenné

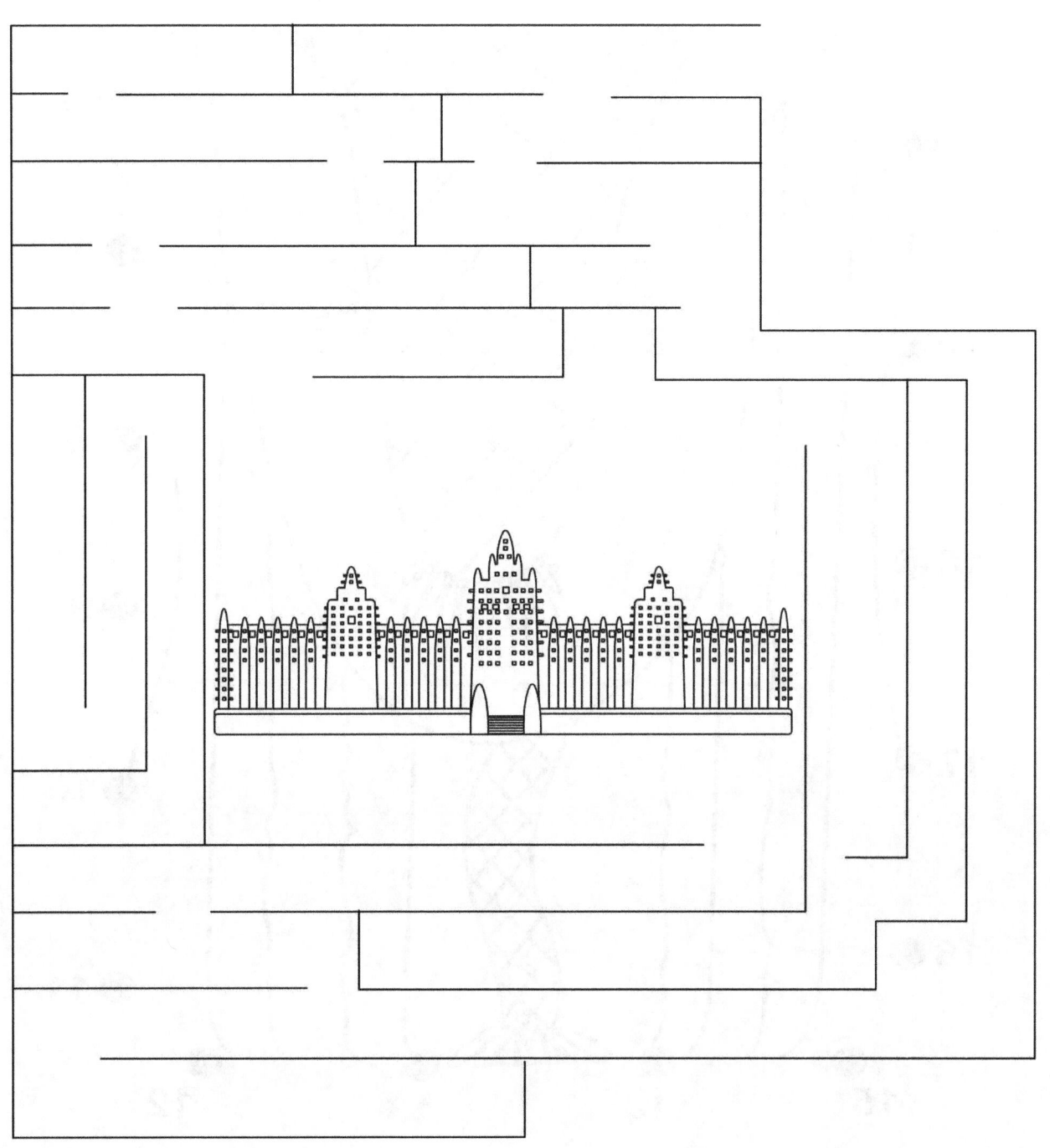

Connect the dots from 1 to 20 to draw a traditional book satchel.

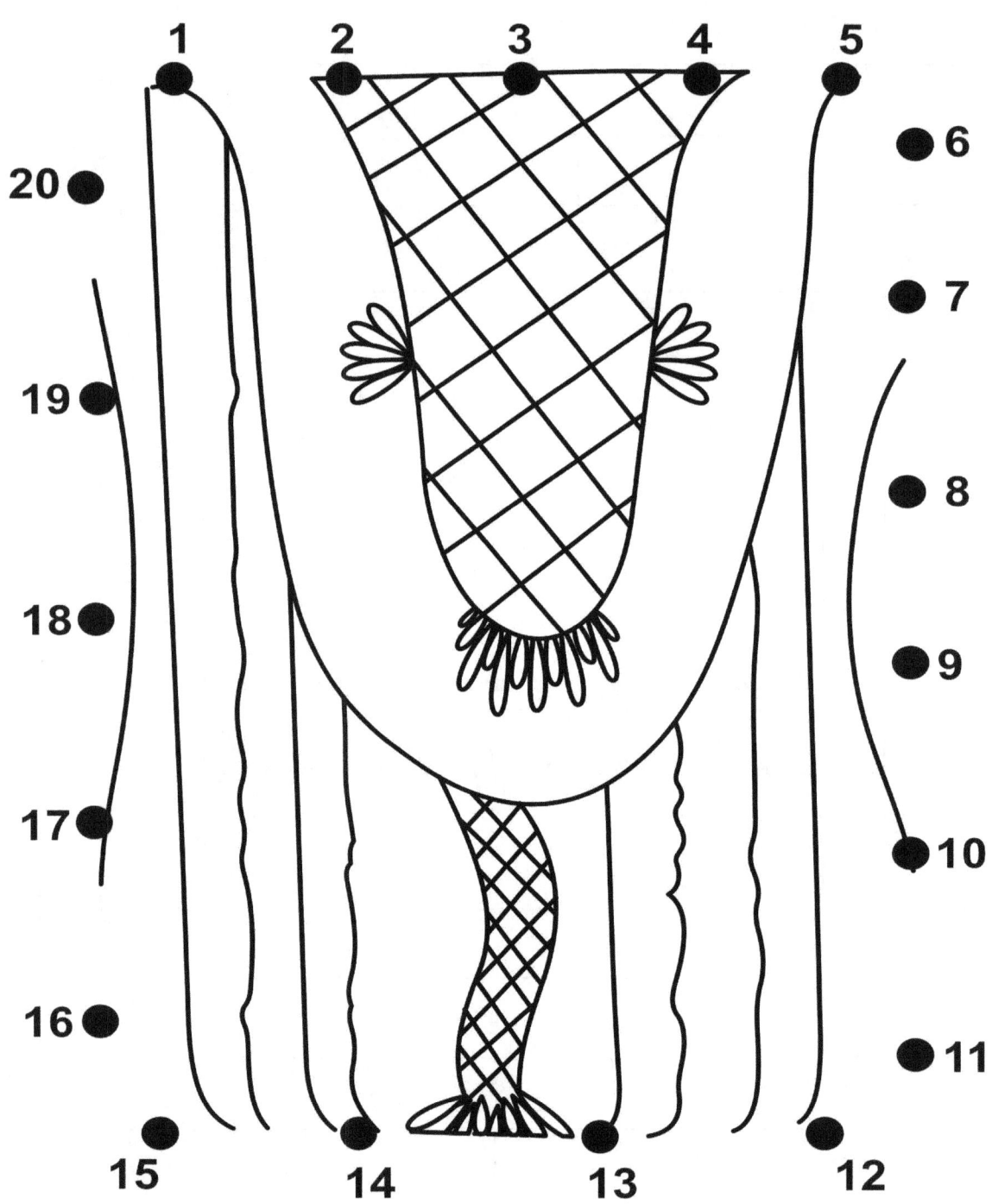

Find the way to the Grand Mosque of Touba.

Map Challenge

Can you label the cities without looking back to the story? You can use an atlas or have an adult help you.

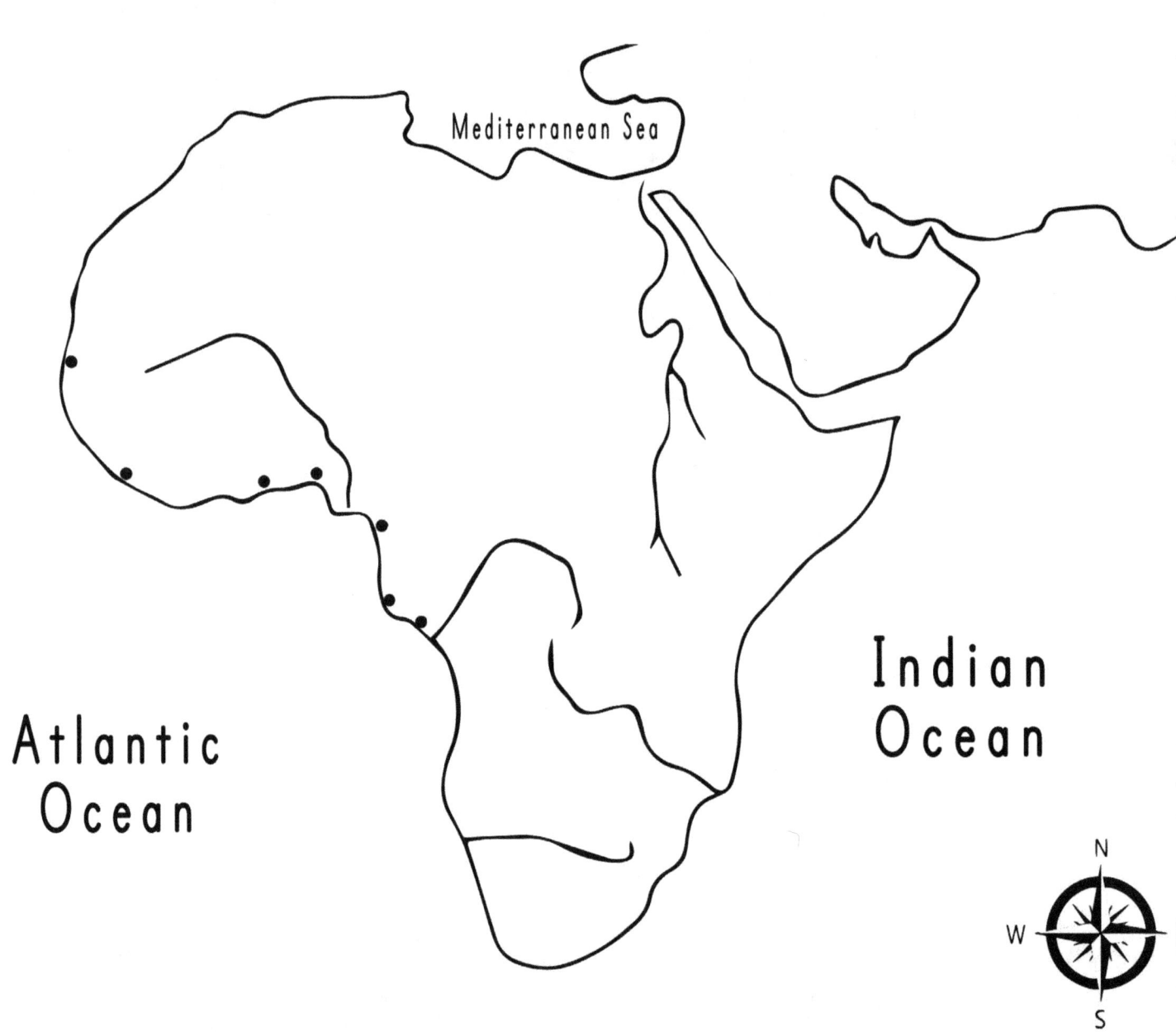

Mosque Shadow Matching

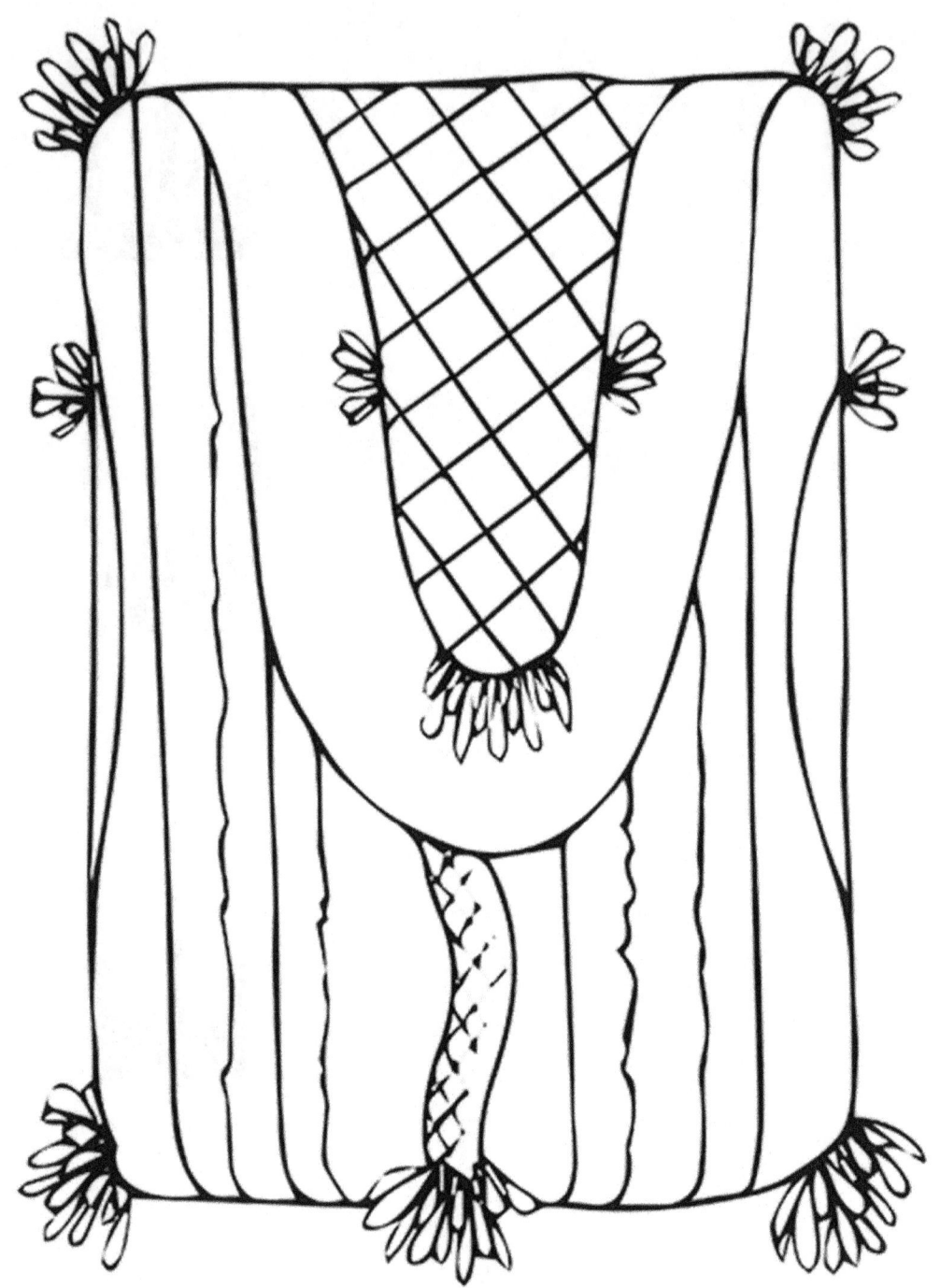

```
L I B R E V I L L E R P T N B W
A I C W I A I C W I A E C O I E
M A Y U M B A D C G X A D C G S
R B W U R M E C C A D C A C I T
A I A Z L C V A E A Z E Z U N A
X G R A N D B A S S A M I P D F
U T M E G G U N T P E G G A E R
M R T E P E C P U Y E T R T P I
R U H B W N O H D R S O O I E C
L C A R R E N S Y N T U S O N A
O K I O I R A I S I O B A N D I
V E R O T O K C C I D A N T E S
E X N R I S R O E H R F P B N H
A I O W N I Y N D A K A R O T A
P L I G G T A W C O T O N O U Y
P E N G L Y T O R P G O D K O K
Y G R A N D M O S Q U E I S K H
```

AXUM **GENEROSITY** **MAYUMBA** **STUDY**
BOOKS **GRAND BASSAM** **MECCA** **TOUBA**
CONAKRY **GRAND MOSQUE** **OCCUPATION** **WARMTH**
COTONOU **INDEPENDENT** **PEACE** **WEST AFRICA**
DAKAR **LIBREVILLE** **SHAYKH** **WRITING**
EXILE **LOVE**

Glossary

Blessed Prophet
His name is Muhammad, a holy man who taught love of God, justice, and kind words and actions.

Colonize
To take control of someone else's land without their permission.

Establish
To set up a thing or place.

Foundation
The supporting structure of a building.

Grand Mosque
The main gathering space for prayer in a community.

Independent
Not needing to rely on anyone else.

Inspired
Filled with the desire to do something great.

Mercy
A great amount of kindness, love and care.

Privy Council
A special court in French controlled lands.

Satchel
A bag usually used for carrying books that is carried on the shoulder by a

long strap.

Satisfied
Content, having enough.

Scholar
A person who is trained in teaching the love of God.

Shackled
To be chained at the ankles and/or wrists.

Shaykh
A man who is trained in teaching the love of God. (fem. Shaykha)

Further Reading for Parents and Teachers

Babou, A Cheikh. Fighting the Greater Jihad: Amadu Bamba and the Founding of the Muridiyya of Senegal, 1853–1913 Athens: Ohio University Press, 2007.

Ngom, Fallou. Muslims Beyond the Arab World: The Odyssey of Ajami and the Muridiyya New York: Oxford University Press, 2016.